Marriage Changes Everything

By Dan Peterson

Suddenly you're sleeping with a relative..

This is a work of fiction. It is a compilation of anecdotes, stories, and jokes. Names, characters, places, and incidents either are the product of the author's imagination or are used fictitiously, and any resemblances to actual persons, living or dead, tall or short, smart or stupid, are entirely coincidental.

Table of Contents

Chapter 1. The Dating Game

My wife was working at a greeting card and gift shop, and she received a call from a young girl who had ordered wedding invitations just two weeks before. The girl wanted to know if it was too late to make a few changes on the invitations. My wife told the young girl to give her the updated information and she would call the printing company. "Okay," the young girl said. "It's just a different date, a different church and a different guy."

Tony had just returned from two weeks of vacation. As soon as he returned he asked his boss for two more weeks off to get married. "What!" shouted the boss? "I can't give you more time now. Why didn't you get married while you were off?" "Are you nuts?" Tony replied. "That would have ruined my whole vacation."

Claudette visited a fortune-teller. "Two men are in love with me," she says. "Please tell me who will be the lucky one?" The fortune teller answers, "Todd will marry you. Andre will be the lucky one."

At a country-club party a young man was introduced to an attractive girl. Immediately he began flattering her. The girl liked the young man, but she was amazed when after 30 minutes he seriously proposed marriage. "Look," she said. "We only met a half hour ago. How can you be so sure? We know nothing about each other.""You're wrong," the young man declared. "For the past five years I've been working in the bank where your father has his account.

Susan hadn't been dating for about two years, and she finally inserted an ad in the classifieds: "Husband Wanted". The very next day she received a hundred and fourteen phone calls and over two hundred and sixty seven e-mails. They all said the same thing: "You can have mine."

I asked my friend Jason how it is that he never married. He replied, "Well, I guess I just never met the right woman ... I guess I've been looking for the perfect girl." "Oh, come on now," I said, "Surely you have met at least one girl that you wanted to marry." "Yes, there was one girl .. once. I guess she was the one perfect girl .. the only perfect girl I really ever met. She was just the right everything .. I really mean that she was the perfect girl for me." "Well, why didn't you marry her?" I asked. "She was looking for the perfect man," he answered.

My niece was recently engaged to a kid named Ted. She went to her mother and said, "I've found a man just like father!" Her mother smartly replied, "So what do you want from me, sympathy?"

"Andrew," she whispered, "will you still love me after we are married?" He considered this for a moment and then replied, "I think so. I've always been especially fond of married women."

Jay walks into a jewelry store to buy his girlfriend an engagement ring. Looking behind the glass case, he comes across an exquisite band with a monster-sized rock in its center. "Excuse me sir," Jay says to the salesman. "How much is this ring?""Ah, that's a beautiful piece," the salesman replies. "It goes for $6,750.""You're kidding!" Jay exclaimed. "That's a lot of money!""Yes, but a diamond is forever." "Perhaps," Jay replied, "But my marriage won't last that long!"

A girl I work with named Angela just announced that she was engaged, so I offered her some advice. "The first ten years of marriage are the hardest," I told her. "How long have you been married?" She asked. "Ten years," I replied.

Shannon went shopping with three of her girlfriends and after a day at the mall she was driving all of them home, she passed the pharmacy. She suddenly realized that she had forgotten to pick up her birth control pills. She immediately turned the car around and rushed into the pharmacy and gave her prescription to the pharmacist. "Please fill this immediately," she said. "I've got people waiting in my car!"

Three weeks before her wedding day, Joanna called her minister. "Reverend," she wailed, "John and I had a dreadful fight!" "Calm down, my child," said the minister, "it's not half as bad as you think. Every couple I know has had a few fights just before the marriage. You're both nervous about the wedding, it's normal for this to happen. Things will work out, they always do. "I know, I know!" said Joanna. "But what am I going to do with the body?"

Janet was trying to teach her daughter Linda how to cook a few simple meals before she got married. Linda just wasn't set out to be a cook. After burning a cake and getting spaghetti stuck to the pan, she finally told her mother, "I read recipes the same way I read science fiction. I get to the end and think, "Well, that's not going to happen."

Chapter 2. Newlyweds

Upset over a newlywed squabble with my husband, I went to my mother to complain. Trying to console me, my dad said that men are not all like this all the time. "Nonsense," I said. "Men are good for only one thing!" "Yes," my mother interjected, "but how often do you have to parallel park?"

All eyes were on Julia as her father escorted her down the aisle. They reached the altar and the waiting groom; Julia kissed her father and placed something in his hand. The guests in the front pews responded with ripples of laughter. Even the minister smiled broadly. As her father gave her away in marriage, Julia gave him back his credit card.

Jesse went up to a perfume counter and asked for a bottle of Chanel no.5. He told the girl he just got a raise at work and he wanted to get something nice for his new wife. "a little surprise, eh?" smiled the clerk. "You bet," answered Jesse. "She's expecting a cruise."

Megan was a newlywed who was a bit shy and didn't want to be seen as a honeymooner. So when she and her husband pulled up to the hotel, she asked him if there was any way that they could make it appear that they had been married a long time. He responded, "Sure. You carry the suitcases!"

A young man staggered into the small town bakery one cold, wet, and stormy morning. "Thank heavens you are open," he gasped. "Do you have fresh double chocolate muffins?" When the baker nodded, a huge smile broke out on the young man's face. "It's worth the trip, and then she'll be so happy. It will make her day!" The baker nodded with understanding. "Are these for your mother, then?" he asked. "No, they are for my wife! Do you think my mother would send me out on a day like this?"

Bethany was saying, "My husband is such a mess-maker that you can't imagine. He doesn't put anything in its place; I am always going around the house organizing things." Her friend Erica said, "Take a tip from me. The first week after we were married I told my husband firmly, 'Every glass and plate that you take, wash when you are done and put back in its place.'" Bethany asked, "Did it help?" Erica said, "I don't know. I haven't seen him since."

When my sister got married, she asked to wear my mother's wedding dress. The day she tried it on for the first time I was sitting with Mother in the living room as Andrea descended the stairs. The gown was a perfect fit on her petite frame. Mother's eyes welled with tears. I put my arm around her. "You're not losing a daughter," I reminded her in time-honored fashion. "You're gaining a son." "Oh, forget about that!" she said with a sob. "I used to fit into that dress!"

My brother in law Jason was a police officer in a small town and he stopped a motorist who was speeding down Main Street. He didn't have his driver's license with him, and he had no other identification. "Officer," the man began, "I can explain.""No explanation needed!" Jason snapped. "I'm going to let you cool your heels in jail until the chief gets back." "But, officer, I have to tell you something." The man tried again. "Just keep quiet! You're going to jail and I'm not interested in what you have to say!" the officer barked. A few hours later Jason looked in on his prisoner and said, "Lucky for you that the chief is at his daughter's wedding. He'll be in a good mood when he gets back." "Don't count on it," answered the fellow in the cell. "I'm the groom."

Jeremy sought to console his bride, who was crying on the sofa. "Beth," he implored, "believe me, I never said you were a terrible cook. I merely pointed out that our garbage disposal has developed an ulcer."

My wife and I got stuck going to a wedding of a relative of hers that I didn't like in the first place. The groom got all choked up and shed a few tears when they exchanged vows.. My wife leaned over to me and whispered, "Why didn't you cry at our wedding?" "I would have," I replied, "if I'd known what was in store for me."

At that same wedding reception, the groom stood to say a few words. He turned to his bride's mother. "You've given me a gift," he began, "a gift that..." Here he paused, a pause that grew in length. "That you can't return!" his mother-in-law completed.

Tony's wife wasn't very attractive, but then he was no oil painting, either. After the wedding ceremony, Tony asked the pastor how much the cost was. "Just give me what you think it is worth to have this lady for your wife," replied the Reverend. Tony looked at his wife, and handed the pastor $50. The pastor looked at Tony's wife and gave him $45 change.

A man came into a gun shop and asked to see a shotgun. The clerk, seeing that the customer was obviously very wealthy showed him a Belgian handcrafted mother of pearl inlay weapon and demonstrated its fine points. It's a bargain at $20,000. The customer says, "No, not quite what I need." Then the clerk brings out an English model and shows off its fine points. It's a steal at only $7,500. The customer says, "No, I don't need anything that fancy." The clerk, disappointed, shows the customer a Winchester 'over and under' mass production model. And it's only $129.95. The customer says, "That will do nicely. After all, it is an informal wedding."

Jason and Kate got married and left on their Honeymoon. When they got back Kate immediately called her mother, who asked, "How was the honeymoon?" Oh mama, she replied, "The honeymoon was wonderful! It was so romantic." But then suddenly she burst out crying. Mama, as soon as we returned, Jason starting using the most horrible language, things I'd never heard before! I mean all these 4-letter words! You've got to come get me and take me home...Please mama!" "Kate, ..Calm down! Now tell your mama what could be so awful? What 4-letter words?" "No mama, don't make me repeat them," she wept. "I'm so embarrassed, they are just too awful." "Tell me Kate, I need to know if you want mama to come and get you."Still sobbing, Kate replied, "Wash, Cook, Iron and words like that.

When our first girl was born, my wife and I named our daughter Alexis. It's a beautiful name, and it's very fitting. After putting her through four years of college and paying for her wedding we've finally realized that if we didn't have her, we could have afforded one.

Andrea had begun to suspect that her husband was cheating on her. He would come home late when she knew he wasn't' working. She started following him when he left the house at night and started reading the text messages that were left on his phone. She would check them when he was in the shower. After months of detective work she finally found evidence of an affair. When she confronted him, he denied everything. And he said it would never happen again.

It was only a short week after my good friend Curtis was married, that he confided in me "I've discovered the only difference between my wife and Charles Manson is that Manson has the decency to look like a nut case when you first meet him."

Chapter 3. It Could Be Worse

"Darling, I would like to ask you a question," said my wife. "Go ahead... I will answer as honestly as I can," I replied. "How would you describe the last fifteen years of our life?" "I would say that we have a strange and wonderful relationship," I said. "Oh, darling," she commented," such a beautiful thing to say! But why do you call it 'strange and wonderful?" "Because you're strange," I remarked, "and I am wonderful!"

Carol was just falling off to sleep when Dwight nudged her and said the telephone was ringing. At this hour it was probably for her, he said, closing his eyes. Carol rolled out of bed and went into the kitchen to answer the phone. When she returned, Dwight was asleep. She woke him."Wasn't for me, after all," she said. He crawled out of bed and pulled on a robe and started walking to the kitchen. Then Carol added, "It was a wrong number."

Barney bought his new colleague, Peter, home for dinner. As they arrived at the door his wife rushed up, threw her arms around Barney and kissed him passionately. Peter exclaimed, "You must have a fantastic marriage if your wife greets you like that after all those years." Barney replied, "Don't be fooled! She only does it to make the dog jealous."

Trying to control my dry hair, I treated my scalp with olive oil before washing it. Worried that the oil might leave an odor, I washed my hair several times. That night when I went to bed, I leaned over to my husband and asked, "Do I smell like olive oil?" "No," he said, sniffing me. "Do I smell like Popeye?"

Morris and his wife, who was eight months pregnant, were shopping in crowded mall. They had been trading humorous insults for most of the evening Morris decided that he was going to really get her. He announced in a loud voice that, "If you don't stop insulting me I'm not going to marry you!" He was disappointed that only a few people around them reacted but his wife managed to bring down the house when she responded, "That's ok, I won't tell you who the father is!"

My Parents had not been out together in quite some time. One Saturday, as Mom was finishing the dinner dishes, my father was standing behind her. "Would you like to go out, girl?" he asked. Not even turning around, my mother quickly replied, "Oh, yes, I'd love to!" They had a wonderful evening, and it wasn't until much later that Dad finally confessed that his question had actually been directed to the family dog, who was lying near Mom's feet on the kitchen floor.

When my wife and I went up to New England a couple of years ago we decided to stay in one of those quaint little inns. The clerk at the inn asked me if we wanted a room with a shower or a tub. "What's the difference?" I asked. "Well, sir, in a tub, you can sit down."

I've been married almost 40 years and I think one of the greatest things about marriage is that as a husband, I can say just about anything I want to around the house. Of course, no one pays the least bit of attention.

One evening Mark, thinking he was being funny, said to his wife Linda, "Perhaps we should start washing your clothes in 'Slim Fast". Maybe it would take a few inches off of your butt!' Linda was not amused, and decided that she simply couldn't let such a comment go unrewarded. The next morning Mark took a pair of underwear out of his drawer. "What the heck is this?" he said to himself as a little 'dust' cloud appeared when he picked them up. "Linda!" he hollered into the bathroom, "Why did you put talcum powder in my underwear?" She replied with a snicker. "Mark, it's not talcum powder; it's Miracle Grow!"

One night Alice was in the kitchen cooking and asked her husband, "Do you want some dinner?" George said, "Sure! What are my choices?" Alice replied, "Yes or no."

Allie was pushing his shopping cart around the supermarket when he collided with a young guy's cart. Allie says to the young guy, "Sorry about that. I'm looking for my wife, and I guess I wasn't paying attention to where I was going. "The young guy says, "That's OK. It's a coincidence. I'm looking for my wife, too. I can't find her and I might be a little late for work."Allie says, "Well, maybe we can help each other. What does your wife look like?" The young guy says, "Well, she is 24 yrs old, tall, with blonde hair, blue eyes, long legs, and she's wearing very tight white shorts, with a halter top. What does your wife look like?" Allie says..... "Doesn't matter --- let's look for yours."

I had some of the nicest neighbors one time named Maxwell and Angela. Angela was a true Southern Belle if there ever was one. We were over their house having a few drinks and her husband and I were laughing at a sexist joke and my wife said, "Men are all alike!" Angela smiled coyly and said, "Men are all Ah like too."

Since my purchases came to $19.06, I handed the cashier a twenty. "Do you have six cents?" she asked. "Sorry," I said after fishing around my pockets, "I have no cents." "Finally after all these years," my wife muttered, "he admitted it."

My wife and I have worked hard and sacrificed because we want our children to have all the things we couldn't afford. Then we want to move in with them.

As I serviced an alarm system at a jewelry store recently, the saleswoman let me know that the store was having a 20 percent off sale. "I bet your girlfriend would love it if you bought her something." she suggested. "I don't have a girlfriend," I answered. "No girlfriend? Why don't you have a girlfriend?" I told her "My wife won't let me.

Chris was adjusting his tie in the mirror before an awards dinner and he asked his wife, "Marianne, how many great men do you think there are in the world today?" "One less than you think," she replied.

Ann and Tom were invited to join friends for an evening out that was over an hour's drive away. It was an elegant restaurant and the atmosphere was great, but Ann remembered that the last time she'd eaten there, her entree was tasteless, unevenly heated, and the meal wasn't worth it. When she reminded Tom why she didn't want to go, Tom was supportive. "You're right Ann, if we want a lousy meal, we don't have to drive so far," he said. "We can just stay here and you can cook."

Rick walked into his friend's Daryl's office, he found him sitting at his desk, looking very depressed. "Hey, what's up with you?" he asks. "Oh, it's my wife," replied Daryl sadly. "She's hired a new secretary for me." "Well, nothing wrong in that. Is she blonde or brunette?" Daryl replied, "Neither, He's bald."

Dan goes to see his supervisor in the front office. "Boss," he says, "we're doing some heavy house-cleaning at home tomorrow, and my wife needs me to help with the attic and the garage, moving and hauling stuff." "We're short-handed, Dan" the boss replies. "I can't give you the day off." "Thanks, boss," says Dan "I knew I could count on you!"

Frank and his wife were involved in a petty argument, both of them unwilling to admit they might be in error. "I'll admit I'm wrong," the wife told Frank in an attempt to end the argument, "if you'll admit I'm right." He agreed and, like a gentleman, insisted she go first. "I'm wrong," she said. With a twinkle in his eye, Frank responded, "You're right!"

About 6 months ago, someone stole one of my credit cards. I don't know how they stole it, and I have no idea who stole it, but I haven't turned them in. They spend less on the credit card than my wife.

Maurice and his wife were lying in bed when he noticed she was reading a book entitled, "What 20 Million American Women Want." He grabbed the book out of her hands and started thumbing through the pages. She was a little annoyed. "Hey, what do you think you're doing?" He calmly replied, "I just wanted to see if they spelled my name right."

Shannon was a great cook but she was anything but a tidy housekeeper. It didn't bother her much until one evening when her husband called from the hall, somewhat dismayed: "Honey, what happened to the dust on this table? I had a phone number written on it."

Rob got into his old work clothes one Saturday morning and set about all the chores Pam had been urging him to do. He cleaned the garage, and was halfway through mowing the lawn when a woman pulled up in the driveway and called out her window, "Say, what you get for yard work?" Rob answered, "The lady who lives here lets me sleep with her."

Michael worked two jobs and barely was home except to eat and go to sleep. Sara would mow the lawn and wash the cars and take care of chores around the house. When Michael mentioned that he heard that a new car wash was opening up in their neighborhood, Sara was thrilled, "How convenient," she said. "I can walk to it!"

I was browsing in an antique shop in New Hampshire when the man next to me struck up a conversation. Just as he was telling me that his wife was getting carried away with her shopping, a brief power shortage caused the lights to flicker overhead. "That," he sighed, "must be her checking out now

If there is one thing that I've learned from marriage, it's that no matter how happily a woman may be married, it always pleases her to discover that there is a nice man out there who wishes that she were not.

Kurt and his wife Betty would often take car trips from Vermont to Canada. One holiday season they were stopped at the border on the way home, where the guard asked Kurt the value of any goods they would be taking back with them. Kurt paused to think of the value of everything they had with them. "Never mind," the guard said, "what's the most expensive thing in your car?" Without hesitation, Kurt replied, "My wife."

I was standing outside work drinking a cup of coffee with a friend, and I saw this woman in a tight black dress, and I said, "She looks dressed to kill." My friend Marvin chipped in, "She probably cooks the same way."

Jim was bringing the Christmas decorations up from the basement and start decorating the house and tree. During one trek up the stairs, heavily laden with boxes, he slipped and luckily only fell about two steps before landing square on his behind. Joan heard the noise and yelled, "What was that thump?" "I just fell down the stairs," he explained. "Anything broken?" asked Joan, and Jim replied, "No, I'm fine." There was just a slight pause before he heard Joan say, "No, I meant my decorations? Are any of them broken?"

My Dad was always frugal with a dollar, and if he was there when she was shopping, he had a sure fire way to keep my Mom from buying an outfit... When she tried it on, he said, "I love that middle-aged look it gives you."

Amy landed a good job with an accounting firm, and after a while she got a generous raise. The day she found out about it, her husband Travis picked her up from work and they stopped for ice cream. As they continued home, Amy blurted out, "Isn't it hard to believe that I have a job that pays this much money?" Just then, she went to toss the last of her ice cream cone out the window. However, the window was closed, and it smacked against the glass. Travis replied calmly, "Yes."

My wife and I were in bed late one night, and we watching an episode of 'Who Wants to Be a Millionaire' that she had recorded earlier. I turned to her and suggested we could get intimate. Her answer was "No". Then I said, "Is that your final answer?" She didn't even look at me this time, simply saying "'yes." So I said, "Then I'd like to phone a friend."

Claudia was in her bath robe, looking at herself in the bedroom mirror. She is not happy with what she sees and says to her husband, ' "I feel horrible; I look old, fat and ugly. I really need you to pay me a compliment." The husband replies, 'Your eyesight's damn near perfect. '

Judy was trying hard to get the ketchup out of the jar. She was banging her palm against the bottom of the bottle with little success. During her struggle the phone rang so she asked her 4-year-old daughter to answer the phone. "Mommy can't come to the phone to talk to you right now. She's hitting the bottle."

I'd have to say my mother is very possessive. Last night she calls me up and says, "You weren't home last night. Is something going on?" I say, "Yeah, Mom. I'm cheating on you with another mother."

Chapter 4. Married With Children

When I was a child, I remember my Mom telling me, "Danny, when you grow up, you can have any girl you please." As I became older, I learned the sad fact was that I could not please any of them.

Larry came into work one day with a fistful of cigars and started passing them out left and right to celebrate the birth of his son. He was beaming with joy. "Congratulations, Larry," said the boss. "How much does the baby weigh?" "Four and a half pounds," reported the father proudly. "Gee, that's kind of small." "What did you expect?" retorted Larry indignantly. "We've only been married three months."

A little girl says, "Daddy, I wish I had a little sister." Trying to be funny, the daddy says, "Honey, you do have a sister." "I do?" questions the confused youngster. "Sure," responds the dad, "You just don't see her because when you are coming in the front door, she is always leaving through the back door." The little girl gave this a few moments thought and remarked, "You mean like my other Daddy does?"

After my mom bought us a pet hamster, after we promised we would take care of it, Mom, as usual, ended up with the responsibility. One evening, exasperated, she asked us, "How many times do you think that hamster would have died if I hadn't looked after it?" After a moment, I replied quizzically, "Er.... Once?"

One day when I was about six years old I walked around the house and I was looking very unhappy. My dad couldn't help but notice. He asked, "Danny, what's wrong?" I said, "I just can't get along with your wife."

Amy was seven years old and she went into her mother's bedroom because she couldn't sleep, and she asked her mother to tell her a bedtime story. Her mother wasn't thrilled with the request. She said, "It's almost two in the morning." "I know, Mommy, but I'd love to hear a story." The mother said, "Lie down in bed with me. We'll wait for your father to come home and he'll tell us both a good one!"

When I was small I saw a program on TV and afterwards I asked my father, "Is it true Dad that in some parts of Africa a man doesn't know his wife until he marries her?" My dad replied, "That happens in every country, son."

Our son Joey's teacher sent a note home to us stating, "Joey seems to be a very bright boy, but spends too much of his time thinking about sex and girls." My wife wrote the teacher back the next day, "If you find a solution, please let me know. I have the same problem with his father."

Lourdes was a Sunday school teacher and she was teaching her class about the difference between right and wrong. "All right children, let's take another example," she said. "If I were to get into a man's pocket and take his billfold with all his money, what would I be?" a little boy raises his hand, and Lourdes asked him if he knew the answer. With a confident smile he blurts out, "You'd be his wife!"

Ellen asked her mother, 'How did the human race appear?' Her mother answered, 'God made Adam and Eve, and they had children, so all mankind was made.' Two days later Ellen asked her father the same question. Her father answered, 'Many years ago there were monkeys from which the human race evolved.' Ellen was confused so she returned to her mother and said, 'Mom how is it possible, you told me the human race was created by God, and Dad said they developed from monkeys?' Her mother answered, 'Well, dear, it is very simple. I told you about my side of the family and your father told you about his.'

Let's just walk up the hill to the terminal, rather than wait for the bus," I suggested to my two young sons. Much to their displeasure, we began our walk. After a while, my seven-year-old son asked: "Mom, why do you always make the decisions?" "Because I'm an adult," I said. "When you become an adult, you'll make the decisions." He thought for a few seconds, and then said: "No, I won't. Then I'll have a wife."

Being a curious kid, I asked my mother, "Do all fairy tales begin with, 'Once upon a time"? "My mother answered, "No, Dan. Once in a while they begin with 'I'll be working late at the office tonight." "Does Dad tell you fairy tales like that?" "He used to." I asked, "What made him stop?" "One day he told me he'd be working late, and I said, 'Can I depend on that?'"

I was probably about ten years old when I went up to my father and asked, "Dad, I know that babies come from mommies' tummies, but how do they get there in the first place?" After my dad hemmed and hawed awhile, I finally spoke up, "You don't have to make something up, Dad, and it's okay if you don't know the answer."

Chapter 5. In Sickness And In Health

It was the third day my husband, Joe, had been in the intensive care unit following his fifth surgery for the removal of most of his remaining small intestine. The surgery took many more hours than expected. Joe was older and weaker, and he wasn't responding. As I sat beside his bed, two nurses tried repeatedly to get him to cough, open his eyes, and move a finger - anything to let them know he could hear them. He didn't respond. I sat praying to God to please help Joe respond - any sign that he might survive. Finally, one of the nurses turned to me and suggested that perhaps if she knew something personal about our family, she could try to stimulate his response with that knowledge. She said, "Maybe you, as his daughter, could help us with such information." I smiled and said, "I'll be happy to give you personal information, and thank you for the compliment, but I'm his wife of forty-three years, not his daughter, and we're about the same age." The nurse looked at me and said, "The entire staff thought you were his daughter and had even commented how wonderful they thought it was that his daughter was with him all the time." As they were expressing how I looked so young, a little cough came from my husband, and we all turned to stare at him. He didn't open his eyes, but loud and clear he said, "She dyes her hair!"

Ron calls his doctor and tells him that his wife has laryngitis. The doctor said there was nothing he could do to cure it. Ron said, "Cure it? Who said I wanted to cure it. I want to prolong it."

When a physician remarked on my father's high blood pressure, my father said "It comes from my family." "Your mother's side or your father's?" the doctor asked. "Neither," he replied. "It's from my wife's family."   "Oh, come now," I said. "How could your wife's family give you high blood pressure?" He sighed. "You ought to meet them sometime, Doc!"

Brenda, pregnant with her first child, was paying a visit to her obstetrician's office. When the exam was over, she shyly began, "My husband wants me to ask you..." "I know, I know." the doctor said, placing a reassuring hand on her shoulder, "I get asked that all the time. Sex is fine until late in the pregnancy." "No, that's not it at all," Brenda confessed. "He wants to know if I can still mow the lawn."

My wife was in the room with me when I was being examined. She mentioned to the doctor, "My husband has a strange disease," "I think it's from stress and overwork. Every time I start asking him for money, he can't hear me at all." "Well, Mrs. Peterson, it's not a disease—it's a talent."

According to my mother, she and my dad decided to start a family soon after he became an officer in the Air Force. When months went by without success, they consulted the base physician, who chose to examine Mom right then and there. "Please disrobe," he told her. "With him in the room??" she yelled, pointing to my father. Turning to dad, the doctor said, "Captain, I think I found the problem."

Lonnie is talking to the family doctor. "Doc, I think my wife's going deaf." The doctor answers, "Well, here's something you can try to test her hearing. Stand some distance away from her and ask her a question. If she doesn't answer, move a little closer and ask again. Keep repeating this until she answers. Then you'll be able to tell just how hard of hearing she really is." So Lonnie walks in the door and says, "Honey, what's for dinner?" He doesn't hear an answer, so he moves closer to her. "Honey, what's for dinner?" Still she doesn't answer. He repeats this several times, until he's standing just a few feet away from her. Finally, she answers, "For the eleventh time, I said we're having MEATLOAF!"

Joanie was taking her time browsing through everything at a yard sale and said to the woman, "My husband is going to be very angry when he finds out I stopped at a yard sale." "I'm sure he'll understand when you tell him about all the bargains," the woman replied. "Normally, yes," Joanie said. "But he called me and told me he fell off a ladder, and he's waiting for me to take him to the hospital."

Matt and his wife Sarah walked into a dentist's office. Matt said to the dentist, "Doc, I'm in one heck of a hurry. I have two buddies sitting out in my car waiting for us to go play golf, so forget about the anesthetic, I don't have time for the gums to get numb. I just want you to pull the tooth, and be done with it! We have a 10:00 AM tee time at the best golf course in town and its 9:30 already... I don't have time to wait for the anesthetic to work!' The dentist thought to himself, "My goodness, this is surely a very brave man asking to have his tooth pulled without using anything to kill the pain." So the dentist asks him, "Which tooth is it sir?" Matt turned to his wife and said, "Open your mouth Sarah, and show him.

Anna was very pregnant, and it was rotten luck when, several days before her due date, her husband fell off a ladder, and he sprained both ankles and was restricted to crutches. So when Anna went into labor and he couldn't drive, she took the wheel, stopping every time she had a contraction. Finally, they got to the hospital. She dropped him at the maternity entrance, and he hobbled off to the admitting desk, where the nurse told him to go to the emergency room. No, it's my wife," he told her. "She's in Labor." "Where is she?" the nurse asked. "She's parking the car and bringing in the bags."

Larry was just waking up from anesthesia after surgery, and his wife was sitting by his side. His eyes fluttered open and he said, 'You're beautiful.' Then he fell asleep again. His wife had never heard him say that before, so she stayed by his side. A few minutes later his eyes opened and he said, 'You're cute.' The wife was disappointed because instead of 'beautiful,' it was now 'cute.' She asked, 'What happened to beautiful?' Larry replied, 'The drugs are wearing off.'

Jeff goes to a psychiatrist and says, "Doctor, you've got to help me. My wife is an extremely beautiful woman, but she is unfaithful to me. Every Friday night, she goes to Maloney's Bar and picks up men. In fact, she sleeps with anybody who asks her! I'm going crazy. What do you think I should do?" "Relax," says the doctor, "take a deep breath and calm down. Now, tell me, where exactly is Maloney's Bar?"

Norman told his doctor that he wasn't able to do all the things around the house that he used to do. When the examination was complete, he said, "Now, Doc, I can take it. Tell me in plain English what is wrong with me?" "Well, in plain English," the doctor replied, "you're just lazy." "Okay," said Norman. "Now give me the medical term so I can tell my wife."

The pastor asked if anyone in the congregation would like to express praise for answered prayers. A lady stood and walked to the podium. She said, "I have praise. Two months ago, my husband, Tom, had a terrible bicycle wreck and his scrotum was completely crushed. The pain was excruciating and the doctors didn't know if they could help him." You could hear a muffled gasp from the men in the congregation as they imagined the pain that poor Tom must have experienced. Tom was unable to hold me or the children," she went on, "and every move caused him terrible pain. We prayed as the doctors performed a delicate operation, and it turned out they were able to piece together the crushed remnants of Tom's scrotum, and wrap wire around it to hold it in place." Again, the men in the congregation were unnerved and squirmed uncomfortably as they imagined the horrible surgery performed on Tom. "Now," she announced in a quavering voice, "thank the Lord, Tom is out of the hospital and the doctors say that with time, his scrotum should recover completely" All the men sighed with relief. The pastor rose and tentatively asked if anyone else had something to say. A man stood up and walked slowly to the podium. He said, "I'm Tom." The entire congregation held its breath. "I just want to tell my wife that the word is sternum."

Alice was patiently waiting at the doctor's office for her husband George to return, when a young man came from the chiropractor's treatment room, and said aloud in the crowded waiting room, "I feel like a new man!" "I do, too," Alice responded, "but I'll probably go home with the same old one."

I took my dad to the doctor's office a few weeks ago. I went into the examining room with him in case he needed help answering any questions, and I wanted to hear what the doctor had to say. "You're in incredible shape," the doctor said to my father. "How old are you again?" "I am seventy eight." My father said. "How do you stay so healthy? You look like a sixty year old." said the doctor.

"Well, my wife and I made a pact when we got married that whenever she got mad she would go into the kitchen and cool off and I would go outside to settle down." My father explained. "What does that have to do with it?" asked the doctor. My father smiled and said, "I've pretty much lived an outdoor life."

A precocious three-year-old girl was waiting with her mother in the doctor's office and after staring for a while she walked up to my pregnant wife and inquisitively asked her, "Why is your stomach so big?" My wife politely replied, "I'm having a baby." With big eyes, the little girl asked, "Is the baby in your stomach?" My wife pointed to her stomach and she answered, "He sure is." Then the little girl, with a puzzled look, asked, "Is it a good baby?" My wife smiled and said, "Oh, yes. It's a real good baby." With an even more surprised and shocked look, she asked, "Then why did you eat him?"

Two old guys were sitting in the park, talking, when the subject turned to getting older. Mark said, "Women have all the luck when it comes to getting older." "What do you mean?" asked Rob. "Well," replied Mark. "I can barely remember the last time I was able to get it up in bed, but my wife is healthier than ever!" "Healthier? How is that?" Rob wondered. "Years ago, when we were younger, almost every night before bed she'd get these terrible headaches." He continued. "Now that we're older, she hasn't had a headache in years."

My wife had not been feeling well and our doctor recommended that she get some exercise and she would definitely feel better. I told my wife to get a trial membership and she didn't listen. She joined an exercise and health spa; she signed up for a year's membership for $300 and on her first day eagerly joined in an exercise class. However, when the class ended she went to the front desk and requested cancellation of her membership. When asked why, she replied, "Your floors are so low that I cannot touch my toes!"

I fell off a ladder at work and I had to be taken to the emergency room. When I called my wife from the hospital, I informed her that I had broken my leg in two places. My wife suggested that I don't go to those places again.

Chapter 6. Maybe He's Had Too Much To Drink

Coming home late after another evening with his drinking buddies, his shoes in left hand to avoid waking his wife, Joel tiptoed as quietly as he could toward the stairs leading to their upstairs bedroom, but misjudged the bottom step in the darkened entryway. As he caught himself by grabbing the banister, his body swung around and he landed heavily on his rump. A whiskey bottle in each back pocket broke and made the landing especially painful. Managing to suppress a yelp, he sprung up, Joel pulled down his pants and examined his lacerated and bleeding cheeks in the mirror of a nearby darkened hallway, then managed to find a large full box of band aids before proceeding to place a patch as best he could on each place he saw blood. After hiding the now almost empty box, he managed to shuffle and stumble his way to bed. In the morning, Joel awakens with screaming pain in head and buttocks to find his wife staring at him from across the room, and hears her say: "You were drunk again last night! Forcing himself to ignore his agony, he looked at her and replied: "Honey, why would you say such a thing?" "Well," she said, "there is the front door left open, the glass at the bottom of the stairs, the drops of blood trailing through the house, and your bloodshot eyes but, mostly.... it's all those band aids stuck on the downstairs mirror!"

Jerry went to the police station pleading to speak with the burglar who had broken into his house the night before. "You'll get your chance in court," said the desk sergeant. "No, no, no!" said Jerry. "You don't understand." "I want to know how he got into the house without waking my wife. I've been trying to do that for years!"

Dana was in no shape to drive, so he wisely left his car parked and walked home. As he was staggering along the sidewalk, he was stopped by a policeman. "What are you doing out here at 2 A.M.?" asked the officer. "I'm going to a lecture, sir." "And who is going to give a lecture at this hour?" the cop asked.
Dana answered "My wife."

Lou is sitting at the bar in his local tavern furiously pounding shots of whiskey. His best friend Tom happens to come into the bar and sees him. "Lou," says the shocked friend, "what are you doing? I've known you for over fifteen years, and I've never seen you take a drink before. What's going on?" Without even taking his eyes off his newly filled shot glass, Lou replies, "My wife just ran off with my best friend." He then throws back another shot of whisky in one gulp. "But," Tom says, "I'm your best friend!" Lou turns to his friend Tom, looks at him through bloodshot eyes, smiles and then slurs, "Not anymore... He is!"

Joe and Bill were sitting in a bar, and Joe was looking really down in the dumps. What's the matter? Bill asked. I don't get it, Joe sighed. The dating scene is so confusing. There are so many damned people you have to please. Like this one woman, she liked me, her mom liked me, but her father hated me. Then there was this other woman, both of her parents really liked me, but she didn't like me. "And then there was this woman I met last night. She absolutely loved me, her parents seemed to really like me too, but her husband couldn't stand me!

I was in a bar last week and I overheard Cecil telling his friend Stu, "I can't break my wife of the habit of staying up until 5 in the morning." "What is she doing?" Stu asked. Cecil answered, "Oh, she's waiting for me to get home."

Bill is sitting at the bar staring morosely into his beer. Doug walks in and sits down. After trying to start a conversation several times and getting only distracted grunts he asks Bob what the problem is. "My wife asked me if I would still love her when she was old, fat and ugly." "That's easy," said Doug. "You just say 'Of course I will'". "Yeah", said Bill, "That's what I did, except I said 'Of course I DO.'"

Rich walks into a bar, orders a drink, gulps it down, looks in his pocket then orders another one. He gulps that one down, looks in his pocket again, and then orders another one. He does this about 7 or 8 more times when the bartender finally asks, "Every time you finish a drink you look in your pocket. What's in your pocket?" Rich replies, "Oh... I have a picture of my wife in there. I drink until she looks good, then I go home."

It was a typical night at the old watering hole. Charlie walked in, took his seat at the bar and ordered a tall one. Then Charlie told his buddy, Bill, "I called the local insane asylum yesterday to check on who has escaped from there recently." Confused by his buddy's comment, Bill asked, "Oh? Why were you wondering about that?" Charlie explained, "Well, somebody married my ex-wife last week."

Walking into the bar, Mike said to Charlie the bartender, "Pour me a stiff one - just had another fight with my wife."
"Oh yeah?" said Charlie, "And how did this one end?" "When it was over," Mike replied, "She came to me on her hands and knees. "Really," said Charlie, "Now that's a switch! What did she say?" She said, "Come out from under the bed, you little chicken."

Last New Year's Eve, things were busy at the Strange Brew Pub and it was getting close to midnight. A pretty young lady stood up at the bar and said that it was time to get ready for the countdown. At the stroke of midnight, she wanted every husband to be standing next to the one person who made his life worth living. Well, it was kind of embarrassing. The bartender was almost crushed to death.

Andy was in his neighborhood bar and he notices a woman, always alone, come in on a fairly regular basis. After the second week, he made his move. "No thank you," she said politely. "This may sound rather odd in this day and age, but I'm keeping myself pure until I meet the man I love." "That must be rather difficult," Andy replied. "Oh, I don't mind too much," she said. But, it has my husband pretty upset."

Jake decided to go to the bar and catch the ball game after work. The game went into extra innings, and he had to drive home slowly because he was way too drunk to go anywhere near the speed limit. His wife wasn't too happy when he finally got to the door. "What's your excuse for coming home at this time of the night?" Jake muttered, "I was golfing with friends, my dear." His wife angrily responded, "What? At 2 A.M.?" He replied, "Yes, We used night clubs."

Rich was sitting in the bar, sipping down a few cold beers before going home and was staring at the half full glass, oblivious to anything going on around him. The bartender interrupted him and asked if everything was all right. Rich looked up and said, "I never knew what real happiness was until I got married." The bartender said that was nice, and Rich continued, "And by then, it was too late."

Frank and Buddy were in a bar after work and they are talking about their wives. "My wife is mad at me again," said Frank. "Why?" "I got really drunk at the bar across the street last night and she came looking for me." Buddy asked, "What'd you do?" Frank replied glumly, "I asked her for her phone number."

One Thursday night, Jack had downed several drinks in rapid succession before the bartender became concerned and asked him, "You trying to drown your sorrows, buddy?" "I guess you could say that," Jack replied. "It usually doesn't work, you know." "No kidding, Jack moaned."I can't even get my wife anywhere near the water!"

It was another night that Joel was getting interrogated by his wife. "What do you mean by coming home half drunk?" Joel's angry wife screamed. "It's not my fault I ran out of money." Joel said.

Mike was sitting in his local pub having a cold one, and said, "When we were first married, I would come home from the office, my wife would bring my slippers and our cute little dog would run around barking. Now after ten years it's all different. I come home, the dog brings the slippers and my wife runs around barking." "Why complain?" said his friend Jerry, "You're still getting the same service."

Greg was talking to his friend Ralph at the bar, "I'll bet you have to think twice before you leave your wife alone at night," "I'll say." answered Ralph. "First, I have to think up a reason for going out. Second, I have to think up why she can't go with me."

After the accident, I told the police officer I thought the driver of the other vehicle was drunk, and he left the scene of the accident. When my wife came to pick me up at the police station, I told her the same thing. Then she told me the police had informed her that the other vehicle was a cow.

Get this." said the bloke to his mates, "Last night while I was down at the pub with you guys, a burglar broke into my house." "Did he get anything." his mates asked. "Yeah, a broken jaw, six teeth knocked out, and a pair of broken ribs. The wife thought it was me coming home drunk."

Rachel was in bed with a man who was not her husband Paul and the heat was up high. All of a sudden, they heard a noise downstairs. "Oh my God, your husband is home. What am I going to do?" "Aw, just stay in bed with me. He's probably so drunk, he isn't gonna notice you here with me." The fear of getting caught trying to escape was more powerful than the thought of getting caught in bed with her, so he trusted her advice. Sure enough, Rachel's husband came crawling into bed and as he pulled the covers over him, he pulled the blankets, exposing six feet. "Honey!" he yelled, "What the heck is going on? I see six feet at the end of the bed.""Dear, you're so drunk, you can't count. If you don't believe me, count them again." Paul got out of bed, and counted, "One, two, three, four... By gosh, you're right dear," as he stumbled back into bed.

Jerry was always in trouble with his wife for drinking too much and coming home late. He was at the neighborhood bar having a few drinks with his buddies and he told them he was going to join Alcoholics Anonymous. He thought that if he drank under an assumed name, that maybe his wife wouldn't find out.

Chapter 7. The In-Laws

Standing at the edge of the lake, a man saw a woman flailing about in the deep water. Unable to swim, the man screamed for help. A trout fisherman ran up. The man said, "My wife is drowning and I can't swim. Please save her. I'll give you a hundred dollars."The fisherman dove into the water. In ten powerful strokes, he reached the woman, put his arm around her, and swam back to shore. Depositing her at the feet of the man, the fisherman said, "Okay, where's my hundred dollars?" The man said, "Look, when I saw her going down for the third time, I thought it was my wife. But this is my mother-in-law." The fisherman reached into his pocket and said, "Just my luck. How much do I owe you?"

A husband and wife were shopping when the wife said, "Darling, it's my mother's birthday tomorrow. What shall we buy for her? She would like something electric." The husband replied, "How about a chair?"

Kristopher says to his buddy, "You'll never believe what happened last night." His buddy says. "Well then, tell me what happened." Kristopher says, "Last night the doorbell rang, and when I opened the door, there was my ex-mother-in-law on the front porch. She said, "Can I stay here for a few days?" I said, "Of course, you can," and shut the door."

Charlie was at work talking to his friend Bill and he said, "I love to drive to the mountains and look at birds. It relaxes me and makes me forget about everything." "What about you?" Bill replied, "I love to drive my mother-in-law to the airport."

One year, Roger decided to buy his mother-in-law a cemetery plot as a Christmas gift. The next year, he didn't buy her any gift at all. When she asked him why he didn't get her a gift, he replied, "Well, you still haven't used the gift I bought you last year!"

Yvonne came into our store looking for some big screws to put in her wall, "Our wall clock fell down and almost killed my mother today." She continued, "It fell only seconds after she got up from the couch." I heard her husband mumble, "Damn clock always was slow."

I read a story the other day that a man in New York got himself arrested so he wouldn't have to spend the holidays with his relatives. I thought to myself, 'Why didn't I think of that?

Today I picked up my mother-in-law at the airport. She's getting a little up there. She's at the age where she doesn't remember things too well. So when I saw her I said, "Thanks for coming. Have a nice flight!"

Chapter 8. Don't Mess With Women

When I picked up my Ford Escort at the service station after some minor repairs, I paid $75 by check as usual. A couple of weeks later, I came home from work to find my wife quite upset. She gave me the silent treatment until I figured out why she was so angry. She had noticed the canceled check and, on the memo line I had written "Escort Service."

Joanie hasn't spoken to her husband since the baby was born, all because of a little misunderstanding... She called him at work and said her water had broken, and he called the plumber. And it's been almost twenty years since it happened.

A man and his wife were having some problems at home and were giving each other the silent treatment. The next week the man realized that he would need his wife to wake him at 5: 00 A. M. for an early flight to New York Not wanting to be the first to break the silence, he finally wrote on a piece of paper, "Please wake me at 5: 00 A. M." The next morning the man woke up, only to discover it was 8:30 A. M. and that he had missed his flight. Furious, he was about to go and see why his wife hadn't woken him when he noticed a piece of paper by the bed. It said. . . "It is 5. 00 A. M. wake up!"

It was a cold winter's night, it was snowing and my wife asked me if I wanted to go to the store to pick up a few groceries with her. I put on my boots and a warm coat and I was ready to go with her. Then she asked, "Do you mind if I don't go?"

Gary's wife was sitting by a tent in a clearing on the bank of a river when along came the park ranger and said, "Excuse me ma'am but I need to speak to your husband. Can you tell me where he is?" She replied, pointing to a clump of reeds. "Go over there and look for the pole with a worm on both ends."

At the Christmas party, Amy was talking to her best friend Holly when she noticed something wasn't right. She asked, "Aren't you wearing your wedding ring on the wrong finger?" Holly shrugged when she replied, "Yes, I discovered that I married the wrong man."

Lorraine was more than upset when she met her husband at the door. There was an awful stench of alcohol on his breath and his car was parked diagonally up on the sidewalk. "I assume," she snarled, "that there is a very good reason for you to come waltzing in here at six o'clock in the morning?" "There is," he replied. "Breakfast."

Chapter 9. High Infidelity

"Nice threads, man," commented Marvin when his buddy showed up one day in a snappy new suit. "Where'd you get them?" Gary beamed. "My wife got them for me. Pretty sharp, huh?" "I'll say. What was the occasion?" "Got me," admitted Gary with a cheerful shrug. "I came home from work early the other day and there they were, hanging over the chair in the bedroom."

The young couple were engaged in a most affectionate embrace when they heard the sound of a key in the hotel door. The young lady broke away at once, eyes wide with alarm. "Oh God," she cried, "It's my husband! Quick, jump out the window." The young man, equally alarmed, made a quick step toward the window, and then stopped. "I can't," he said, "we're on the thirteenth floor." "Just jump," cried the young lady in exasperation, "do you think this the right time to be superstitious?"

Jannine was walking along pushing her newborn baby in the carriage when an old friend approached her. The friend leaned over, peering into the carriage said, "What a beautiful baby boy, and he looks just like his father." "I know." replied Jannine, "I just wish he looked more like my husband!"

Wallace was a jealous husband hired a private detective named Jake to check on the movements of his wife. He wanted more than a written report; he wanted video of his wife's activities. A week later, Jake returned with a video. They sat down together to watch it. The quality was perfect, Wallace saw his wife meeting another man! He watched the two of them as they were laughing in the park. He saw them enjoying themselves at an outdoor cafe. He saw them dancing in a dimly lit nightclub. He saw the man and his wife participate in a dozen activities with utter glee. "I just can't believe this," the distraught husband said. Jake said, "What's not to believe? It's right up there on the screen!" Wallace replied, "I can't believe that my wife could be so much fun!"

Ron was sitting quietly watching TV when his wife walked up behind him and whacked him on the head with a magazine. 'What was that for?' he asked. 'That was for the piece of paper in your pants pocket with the name Laura Lou written on it,' she replied. 'Two weeks ago when I went to the races, Laura Lou was the name of one of the horses I bet on,' he explained. 'Oh honey, I'm sorry,' she said. 'I should have known there was a good explanation.' Three days later he was watching a ballgame on TV when she walked up and hit him in the head again, this time with the iron skillet, which knocked him out cold. When he came to, Ron asked, 'What the hell was that for?' 'Your horse called!'

Jack arrived home unexpectedly a day early from a business trip, and he was shocked to discover his wife in bed with his next door neighbor. "Since you are in bed with my wife," Jack shouted, "I'm going over and sleep with yours!" "Go right ahead," was the reply. "The rest will do you good."

Hank finally found the nerve to tell his fiancée that he had to break off their engagement so that he could marry another woman. "Can she cook like I can?" the distraught woman asked. "Not on her best day." Hank replied. "Can she buy you expensive gifts like I do?" she asked. "No, she's broke." "Well then, is it sex?" "Nope, nobody does it like you, babe." "Then what is it?? What can she do for you that I can't?" "She can sue me for child support!"

It was Ted's birthday and Karen decided to pick up a small present and pay a visit to her husband at the office, just as a surprise. She thought maybe they could go out for lunch. She found him with his secretary sitting in his lap. Without hesitating, he dictated, "...and in conclusion, gentlemen, shortage or no shortage, I cannot continue to operate this office with just one chair."

Aaron and Janice had two beautiful daughters but always talked about having a son. They decided to try one last time for the son they both had always wanted. Janice finally got pregnant and delivered a healthy baby boy. Aaron rushed from work as fast as he could drive to the hospital to see his newborn son. He was horrified to look at the ugliest child he had ever seen. He told his wife, "There's no way in hell that I can be the father of this baby. Look at the two beautiful daughters I fathered! Have you been fooling around behind my back?" Janice smiled sweetly and replied: "Not this time!"

A man and woman were having dinner in a fine restaurant. Their waitress, taking another order at a table a few steps away, suddenly noticed that the man was slowly sliding down his chair and under the table, but the woman acted unconcerned. The waitress watched as the man slid all the way down his chair and out of sight under the table. Still, the woman appeared calm and unruffled, apparently unaware that her dining companion had disappeared. The waitress went over to the table and said to the woman, "Pardon me, ma'am, but I think your husband just slid under the table." The woman calmly looked up at her and said, "No he didn't. He just walked in the door!

Chapter 10. Divorce Court Is Now In Session

After four years of separation, my wife and I finally divorced amicably. I wanted to date again, but I had no idea of how to start, so I decided to look in the personals column of the local newspaper. After reading through all the listings, I circled three that seemed possible in terms of age and interest, but I put off calling them. Two days later, there was a message on my answering machine from my ex-wife. "I came over to your house to borrow some tools today and saw the ads you circled in the paper. Don't call the one in the second column. It's me."

'Mr. Dawson, I have reviewed this case very carefully, ' the divorce Court Judge said, 'and I've decided to give your wife $775 a week,' 'that's very fair, your honor, ' the husband said. 'And every now and then I'll try to send her a few bucks myself.'

A woman in my office, who was recently divorced after years of marriage, had signed up for a refresher CPR course. "Is it hard to learn?" someone asked. "Not at all," my co-worker replied. "Basically you're asked to breathe life into a dummy. I don't expect to have any problems. I did that for 12 years."

Tammy appeared before the judge and said, "I want a divorce." The judge said, "Why do you want a divorce?" She replied, "Because I found out my husband is a terrible lover." The judge asked, "How long have you been married?" "Fourteen years," she replied. "I don't understand. Why did you wait fourteen years to divorce your husband for being a terrible lover?" She said, "Your Honor, until this insurance salesman stopped by my house last week, I didn't know."

Margaret applied for a job in a Florida lemon grove even though she seemed overqualified for the job. "Look Miss," said the foreman, "do you have any experience in picking lemons?" "Well... as a matter of fact, yes !" she replied. "I've been divorced three times."

"Well, Mrs. O'Connor, so you want a divorce?" the lawyer questioned his client. "Tell me about it. Do you have a grudge?" "Oh, no," replied Mrs. O'Connor. "We have a carport." The lawyer tried again. "Well, does the man beat you up?" "No, no," said Mrs. O'Connor, looking puzzled. "I'm always first out of bed." Now desperate, the lawyer pushed on. "What I'm trying to find out is what grounds you have." "Oh...we live in a flat -- not even a window box, let alone grounds." "Mrs. O'Connor," the lawyer said in considerable exasperation, "you need a reason that the court can consider. What is the reason for you seeking this divorce?" "Ah, well now," said the lady, "It's because the man can't hold an intelligent conversation."

As they sat in the café drinking a cup of coffee, Grace confided to her girlfriend, "Howard and I been divorced for four years and now I'm finding out that my ex-husband wants to marry me again." The friend said, "How flattering." Grace replied, "Not really. I think he's after the money I married him for."

Angel went to the bank and applied for a loan. She wasn't familiar with the process and she stated, "I want to apply for a loan; I'm going to divorce my husband." "Oh, we don't give loans for divorces" the customer loan officer said, "We finance loans for mortgages, automobiles, businesses, home improvements...." Angel interrupts her and says "Well, this is certainly a 'Home Improvement.'

Once Michelle's divorce was final, she went to the local Department of Motor Vehicles to have her maiden name reinstated on her driver's license. After a short wait of about two hours, she was finally served. "Will there be any change of address?" inquired the clerk. "No," She replied. "Oh, good," the clerk said, clearly delighted. "You got to keep the house."

"The thrill is gone from my marriage," Bill told his friend Doug. "Why not add some intrigue and danger to your life and have an affair?" Doug suggested. "But what if my wife finds out? She would have me in divorce court in five minutes and I'd lose everything" "Heck, this is a new age we live in, Bill. Go ahead and tell her you're thinking about it!" So Bill went home and said, "Debra, I think an affair will bring us closer together.""Forget it," said his wife. "I've tried that...it never worked."

After fifteen years, enough was enough and Mary decided to get a divorce and she hired an attorney. During the lengthy deposition one of the questions he asked was, "Has your husband lived up to all the things he said before you were married?" Mary replied, "No, He's only lived up to one of them." The attorney asked, "Which one was that?" She said "He said he wasn't good enough for me."

John was talking to his wife the other day as they ate their dinner. He said, "Guess what I heard today?" "What, honey?" she asks. "I heard that the mailman has seduced every woman in our building but one." "Huh," his wife says, "I bet it's that stuck-up Phyllis down the hall." The next day they were in divorce court.

Chapter 11. Women Are Crazy

My wife hasn't been feeling well, so I was worried when she didn't answer her phone. I jumped into the car and raced home, only to find her sitting in her living room calmly watching TV. "Why didn't you answer your phone?" I asked. "I was worried." "Sorry dear. I heard it ringing, but I thought it was on the television." "Oh." I said, relieved. "What were you watching?" "Game of Thrones."

Ruby told her friend, "I ran into my ex-husband last night. Cora inquired, "What in the world happened?" and Ruby explained, "Nothing much...I put it into reverse and hit him again!"

Beverly was chatting with her next-door neighbor. "I feel really good today. I started out this morning with an act of unselfish generosity. I gave a five dollar bill to a bum." "You gave a bum five whole dollars? That's a lot of money to just give away. What did you husband say about it?" "Oh, he thought it was the proper thing to do. He said, 'Thanks.'"

Jeff and his wife are lying in bed, and Jeff looks at his wife and says, "I am going to make you the happiest woman in the world" His wife says, "I will miss you..."

Melissa visited a matchmaker for marriage and requested "I'm looking for a spouse. Can you please help me to find a suitable one?" The matchmaker asked her requirements. "Well, let me see. He needs to be polite, humorous, sporty, knowledgeable, and good at singing and dancing and telling me interesting stories when I need a companion for conversation and be silent when I want to rest." The matchmaker listened carefully and replied, "I understand. You need a television."

Jayne was all visually upset because her husband left her for another woman, and she was plotting the worst revenge possible. She had all these great ideas on what she was going to do to this woman until her friend Caroline advised her, "When some woman steals your husband, I don't there is any better revenge than to let her keep him."

Adam and his wife were considering traveling to Alaska--a trip that he had long dreamed of taking. He kept talking about how great it would be to live in a log cabin, and go fishing every day, and get away from it all. Adam asked, "If we decided to live there permanently, away from civilization, what would you miss the most?" She replied, "You."

My co-workers sympathized as my mother complained that her back was really sore from moving furniture. "Why didn't you wait till your husband got home?" Someone asked. "I could," my mother told the group," but the couch is easier to move if he's not on it."

Lisa goes out shopping with her daughter when she eyes an expensive fur coat. "This year," she says, "I think that I will buy my own present instead of making you and dad shop for me." Her daughter nods in total agreement. "And I think this fur coat would be perfect too." The daughter protests, "But mom, some helpless, poor creature has to suffer so that you can have this." "Don't worry," Lisa says, "your father won't get the bill for a couple of weeks."

Eric was relaxing on the sofa watching the ball game on TV after a hard day at work, when he heard his wife's' voice in the kitchen. "And what would you like for dinner, sweetie? Do you want chicken, beef or lamb?" Surprised, Eric answered, "Thanks! I'd like chicken." His told him, "You're having soup. I was talking to the cat."

Frustrated at always being corrected by John, Jill decided the next time it happened, she would have a comeback. That moment finally arrived, and Jill was ready. "You know," Jill challenged, "even a broken clock is right once a day." John looked at her and replied, "Twice."

Two women were talking at a party, and one said, "Look at that awful-looking man over there... isn't he hideous? I think he must be the most unattractive man I've ever seen in my life!" "That happens to be my husband!" said the second coldly. "Oh dear," said the first, covered in confusion, "I'm so sorry." To which the unfortunate wife replied, "YOU'RE sorry?"

I was covering a register because one of the cashiers was on a break, and a woman was purchasing a gallon of paint and a couple of brushes. As she fumbled for her wallet, I noticed a remote control for a television set in her purse. "So, do you always carry your TV remote?" I asked. "No, "she replied, "but my husband refused to come shopping with me, and I figured this was the most evil thing I could do to him legally."

Debra seriously wanted to find a man who is truly into commitment because she had insecurities. She spent several years and did a lot of research, a lot of digging, and she finally found one, he just happened to be confined in a mental institution.

Women seem to know what's going on in their man's lives almost better than they do. Also known as 'women's intuition,' this sixth sense thing is no myth. Why is this? In the early 80's researchers discovered that women have more connections between the brain's two hemispheres than men do. It's these connections that allow them to put together a puzzle from seemingly unconnectedly pieces. And they go through your stuff while you're in the shower.

When the car engine developed a slight knock, I asked my wife if she had bought a different gas, but she couldn't remember. "You probably got the cheaper gas," I said. "That could account for the way the engine was running." "No, the gas wasn't cheaper!" she replied indignantly. "Well, how much did it cost?" I asked. "It cost the same as always." said my wife. "I told the man to put in the usual twenty dollars worth."

I stopped by to drop off a box of stuffing for our newly married daughter Nina, who was preparing her first Thanksgiving dinner. I noticed the turkey thawing in the kitchen sink with a dish drainer inverted over the bird. I asked why a drainer covered the turkey. Nina turned to me and said, "Mom always did it that way." "Yes," I replied, "but you don't have a cat!"

A bricklayer at Francisco's construction company routinely complained about the contents of his lunch box. "I'm sick and tired of getting the same old thing!" he shouted one day. "Tonight I'll set my wife straight." The next day Francisco could hardly wait until lunch time to hear what happened. "You bet I told her off," the bricklayer boasted. "I said, 'No more of the same old stuff. Be creative!' We had one heck of a fight, but I got my point across." He had indeed. In front of an admiring audience, he opened his lunch box to find that his wife had packed a coconut and a hammer.

Polly walks in a store to return a pair of eyeglasses that she had purchased for her husband a week before. "What seems to be the problem? "I'm returning these glasses I bought for my husband. He's still not seeing things my way."

After my wife and I had a huge argument, we ended up not talking to each other for days. Finally, on the third day, I asked her where my favorite red shirt was. "Oh," she said, "So now you're speaking to me." I was confused, "What are you talking about?" "Haven't you noticed I haven't spoken to you for three days?" she challenged. "No," I said, "I just thought we were getting along."

Chapter 12. Men Are Stupid

One day my housework-challenged husband decided to wash his sweatshirt. Seconds after he stepped into the laundry room, he shouted to me, "What setting do I use on the washing machine?" "It depends," I replied. "What does it say on your shirt?" He yelled back, "University of Oklahoma."

One night, after the couple had retired for the night, the woman became aware that her husband Tony was touching her in a most unusual manner. He started by running his hand across her shoulders and the small of her back. Then he proceeded to run his hand gently down her side, sliding his hand over her stomach, and then he continued on, gently feeling her hips, first one side and the other. Tony stopped abruptly and rolled over to his side of the bed. 'Why are you stopping'? She whispered. Tony whispered back, 'I found the remote'.

Mark heard his wife remark to a lady friend that he was a model husband. He was very proud and happy that his wife would say that. But later that night, he looked the word 'model' up and found that the dictionary defines model as meaning a small imitation of the real thing.

Joe's wife likes to sing. She decided to join the church choir. From time to time she would practice while she was in the kitchen preparing dinner. Whenever she would start in on a song, Joe would head outside to the porch. His wife, with hurt feelings, said, "What's the matter, Joe? Don't you like my singing?" Joe replied, "Honey, I love your singing, but I just want to make sure the neighbors know that I'm not beating you."

While attending a marriage seminar on communication, Ryan and his wife listened to the instructor declare, "It is essential that husbands and wives know the things that are important to each other." He addressed the man, "Can you describe your wife's favorite flower?" Ryan leaned over, touched his wife's arm gently and whispered, "Pillsbury All-Purpose, isn't it?"

I returned home from my ninth business trip of the year with a severe bout of jet lag. As we prepared to go to sleep that night, I wrapped my arms around my wife, gave her a kiss, and announced, "It's good to be in my own bed, with my own wife!"

Mark said, "I'm feeling so depressed today." Linda asked, "Why, Honey?" Mark answered, "It's just that sometimes I feel so alone and useless." Linda replied," Oh, you don't have to feel so alone. A lot of people think you're useless."

Rob absolutely hated his wife's cat and decided to get rid of him one day by driving him 20 blocks from his home and leaving him at the park. As he was getting home, the cat was walking up the driveway. The next day he decided to drive the cat 40 blocks away. He put the cat out and headed home. Driving back up his driveway, there was the cat! He kept taking the cat further and further and the cat would always beat him home. At last he decided to drive a few miles away, turn right, then left, past the bridge, then right again and another right until he reached what he thought was a safe distance from his home and left the cat there. Hours later Rob calls home to his wife: "Pam, is the cat there?" "Yes," she answers, "why do you ask?" Frustrated, Rob answered, "Put that damn cat on the phone, I'm lost and I need directions!"

As Lucy was on the way home from a long and stressful day at the office, her cell phone rang. It was her husband. "Will you be joining me in the whirlpool bath tonight?" he asked. "What a lovely way to spend an evening," She thought. She was about to tell him how considerate he was when he continued, "Because if you're not, I need to start adding more water to the tub."

Bill owned a vintage car that he rebuilt, and he was somewhat reluctant to allow his wife Mary to drive his prize possession even to the corner store which was a mile from the house. After she insisted, he finally relented, cautioning her as she departed, "Remember, if you have an accident, the newspaper will print your age."

On the phone with a golf buddy who has asked him to play, a guy says: "I am the master of my home and can play golf whenever I want. But hold on a minute while I find out if I want to.

Ray said to his wife Ellen one day, "I don't know how you can be so stupid and so beautiful all at the same time." Ellen responded, "Allow me to explain. God made me beautiful so you would be attracted to me; God made me stupid so I would be attracted to you!"

One evening, Marianne drew her husband's attention to the couple next door and said, "Chris, do you see that couple and how devoted they are? He kisses her every time they meet. Why don't you do that?" Chris replied, "I don't know her well enough."

Chip and Elliott are fishing at their favorite lake, just fishing quietly and drinking a few beers. Almost silently, so as not to scare the fish, Chip says, "I think I'm going to divorce my wife - she hasn't spoken to me in over 2 months." Elliott continues slowly sipping his beer, and then thoughtfully says, "You better think it over - women like that are hard to find."

Mark thought it would be nice to bring his wife Linda a little gift. "How about some perfume?" He asked the cosmetics clerk. She showed him a bottle costing $50.00. "That's a bit much," said Mark, so she returned with a smaller bottle for $30.00. "That's still quite a bit," Mark complained. Growing annoyed, the clerk brought out a tiny $15.00 bottle. "What I mean," said Mark "is I'd like to see something really cheap." The clerk handed him a mirror.

Francis walked into a dress shop and told the clerk he wanted to buy an expensive dress for his wife. He didn't go a lot of homework before shopping. The sales clerk asked, "What size?" Francis shrugged blankly. Trying to help, the clerk inquired, "Well then, what are your wife's measurements?" Francis thought for a moment. "Small, medium, and large and in that order."

Stan was reading a newspaper and drinking a coffee. He says to his wife, "You know, honey, I think there might be some real merit to what this article says, and that the intelligence of a father often proves a stumbling block to the son." "Well, thank heaven," said the wife, "at least our James has nothing standing in his way."

Arthur was an unemployed screenwriter who was working hard and awaiting his first big break. One day he comes home to a burned down house. His sobbing wife is standing outside. "What happened, honey?" the man asks. "Oh, Arthur, it was terrible," she weeps. "I was cooking when the phone rang. It was your agent. Because I was on the phone, I didn't notice the stove had caught on fire. It went up in seconds. Everything is gone. I nearly didn't make it out of the house. Poor Fluffy is gone." "Wait! Back up a minute," Arthur says. "My agent called?"

Curious when I found an old roll of film in a drawer, I had them made into prints. I was pleasantly surprised to see that they were of a younger, slimmer me, taken on one of my first dates with my husband. When I showed him the photos, his face lit up. "Wow, look at that!" he said with appreciation. "It's my old Chevy!"

Chapter 13. Better Get A Lawyer

Harley was in court defending a client, and he asked her, "Now would you please tell the Jury the truth. Why did you shoot your husband with a bow and arrow?" His client answered as truthfully as she could, "I didn't want to wake up the children. "

A millionaire informs his attorney, "I want a stipulation in my Will that my wife is to inherit everything, but only if she remarries within six months of my death.""Why such an odd stipulation?" asks the attorney. "Because," he says, "I want someone to be sorry I died."

Stacey phones her husband, Jim, at work for a chat. Jim said, "I'm sorry, but I'm up to my neck in work today." Stacey replied, "But I've got some good news and some bad news for you, dear." Jim responded, "OK, but as I've got no time now, just give me the good news." Stacey gave him the good news, "Well, the air bag works."

Michael was teaching his wife to drive when the brakes suddenly failed on a steep hill. "I can't stop!" she screamed. "What should I do?" "Hold tight," Michael instructed, "And try to hit something cheap."

Chip's barn burned down, and his wife called the insurance company. "We had that barn insured for twenty thousand, and I want my money." The agent replied, "Hold on just a minute, insurance doesn't work quite like that. We will ascertain the value of what was insured and provide you with a new barn of comparable worth." There was a long pause before his wife replied, "Then I'd like to cancel the policy on my husband."

Mario complained to me about having had two unhappy marriages. I was a little confused so I asked him what he meant and he said his first wife divorced him and his second wife wouldn't.

Last week I had lunch with my best friend Ed. I was the best man at his wedding. "Jason" he said, "Holly and I are going to get a divorce". I was stunned. "Why? What happened, you two seem get along so well?" "Well" he said, "ever since we got married, Holly has tried to change me. She got me to stop drinking, smoking, running around at all hours of the night and more. She taught me how to dress well, enjoy the fine arts, gourmet cooking, blues music and how to invest in the stock market." "Are you a little bitter because she spent so much time trying to change you?" I probed. "Nah, I'm not bitter. Now that I'm so improved, she just isn't good enough for me."

Dusty was brought up on charges of bigamy. The judged looked at the docket and said, "Good God, man! You're charged with marrying six women. How could you do such a thing?" "Hey, judge, give me a break," Dusty replied. "I was only trying to find a good one."

A lawyer was trying to console a weeping widow. Her husband had passed away without a will. "Did the deceased have any last words?" asked the lawyer. "You mean right before he died?" sobbed the widow. "Yes," replied the lawyer. "They might be helpful if it's not too painful for you to recall." "Well," she began, "he said 'Don't try to scare me! You couldn't hit the broad side of a barn with that gun.'"

Chris was sitting in his attorney's office. "Do you want the bad news first or the terrible news?" the lawyer said. "Give me the bad news first." "Your wife found a picture worth a half-million dollars.""That's the bad news?" asked Chris incredulously. "I can't wait to hear the terrible news." "The terrible news is that it's of you and your secretary."

My uncle told me about a divorce suit he handled recently. "I think you might as well give your husband a divorce," he advised the wife. "What!" shouted the lady? "I have lived with this bum for twenty years, and now I should make him happy?"

Wes and his wife went for counseling after 15 years of marriage. When asked what the problem was, his wife went into a passionate, painful tirade listing every problem they had ever had in the 15 years they had been married. She went on and on and on: neglect, lack of intimacy, emptiness, loneliness, feeling unloved and unlovable, an entire laundry list of un-met needs she had endured over the course of their marriage. Finally, after allowing this to go on for a sufficient length of time, the therapist got up, walked around the desk and, after asking the wife to stand, embraced and kissed her passionately. The woman shut up and quietly sat down as though in a daze. The therapist turned to Wes and said, "This is what your wife needs at least three times a week. Can you do this? Wes thought for a moment and replied, "Well, I can drop her off here on Mondays and Wednesdays, but on Fridays, I go fishing with my buddies."

I sent this letter to my local newspaper, as much as I hate writing. Dear Editor, 'My wife was about to file for a divorce when she read the article in your paper about the importance of giving second chances in making a marriage work. So after reading your article she changed her mind about our divorce. Effective today, I would like to cancel my subscription to your paper'

Jessica was dazzling redhead and she was thrilled to have obtained a divorce and she was indeed dazzled by the skill and virtuosity of her lawyer, not to mention his healthy income and good looks. In fact, she began to realize that she had fallen in love with him, even though he was a married man. "Oh, Warren," she sobbed at the conclusion of the trial, "isn't there some way we can be together, the way we were meant to be?" Taking her by the shoulders, Warren proceeded to scold her for her lack of discretion and good judgment. "Snatched drinks in grimy bars on the edge of town, lying on the phone, hurried meetings in sordid motels rooms - is that really what you want for us?" "No, no..." she sobbed, heartsick."Oh," said the lawyer. "Well, it was just a suggestion."

Kristen was in court charged with seriously wounding her husband. He was in intensive care but expected to survive. "But why did you stab him over a hundred times?" asked the judge. "Oh, your Honor," Kristen replied, "I didn't know how to switch off the electric carving knife."

Lynette and Sophie had worked together, but they had been out of touch for years until they bumped into each other at the mall one day. Lynette said, "Sophie, it's been so long. I heard you got married." "Yes," said Sophie, "I married a lawyer, and an honest man, too." "Hmmm," said Lynette "isn't that bigamy?"

Eddie and Brittany's marriage was on the rocks and they sought the advice of a marriage counselor. After several visits, the counselor pleaded with them to patch up their differences, but they were adamant. "So," said the counselor, "you know the consequences and you want to part your own separate ways. Remember this. You must divide your property equally." There was a challenging gleam in the Brittany's eye. "What about our three children?" That stumped him. Shrewdly he measured up the situation, and then he came up with an answer. "Go back and live together until your fourth child is born. Then you take two children and your husband takes two."Brittany shook her head. "No, I'm sure that wouldn't work out. If I depended on him, I wouldn't have the three I got."

It was the last day of the murder trial and Leanne was on the witness stand, accused of poisoning her husband. "After you put poison in the coffee, you sat at the breakfast table and watched your husband drink it. Tell me, didn't you feel the slightest bit of pity for him?" the district attorney prompted. "Yes," she replied, "I think there was one moment when I felt sorry for him." "And when was that?" Leann continued, "When he asked for his second cup.

Chapter 14. This Could End Badly

Hey guys, has she ever really forgiven you? Her eyes say, "Maybe," but the lighter fluid in your hair and the match in her hand say, "Not really."

I told my friend Louie that my wife and I were having problems and we had irreconcilable differences. He responded, "What do you mean by that?" I said, "She's melting down her wedding ring to cast it into a bullet.

A woman goes to the police station to report that her husband was missing. "Can you give me a description of him?" asked the officer. "He's short and bald and skinny and wrinkled and wears dentures," answered the woman. "Come to think of it, most of him was missing before he was."

A husband, while he is on a business trip, sends a telegram to his wife: "I wish you were here." However, the clerk at the Telegram office was not such a great typist. The message received by the wife was: "I wish you were her."

A nice, calm, respectable lady went into the pharmacy, walked up to the pharmacist, looked straight into his eyes, and said, "I would like to buy some cyanide." The pharmacist asked, "Why in the world do you need cyanide?" The lady replied, "I need it to poison my husband." The pharmacist's eyes got big and he exclaimed, "I can't give you cyanide to kill your husband. That's against the law! I will lose my license! They'll throw both of us in jail! Absolutely not! You CANNOT have any cyanide!" The lady reached into her purse and pulled out a picture of her husband at a fancy restaurant, having dinner with the pharmacist's wife.
The pharmacist looked at the picture and replied, "Well now, that's different. You didn't tell me you had a prescription."

Joe was walking down the street and he saw a man lying on the sidewalk outside of the beauty parlor, writhing in pain. He asked, "What happened to you?" The man shook his head groggily and rubbed his bruised chin. "Last thing I remember was my wife came out of the beauty salon. I took a look at her and said, 'Well, Honey, at least you tried,' and that was the last thing I remember."

Jennifer and Thomas had a big argument. She yelled at her husband, "You're gonna be really sorry! I'm going to leave you!" Her husband responded, "Make up your mind! Which one is it gonna be?"

Dave was in trouble. He forgot his wedding anniversary. His wife was really angry. She told him ' Tomorrow morning, I expect to find a gift in the driveway that goes from 0 to 200 in less than six seconds AND IT BETTER BE THERE!! The next morning Dave got up early and left for work. When his wife woke up she looked out the window and sure enough there was a box gift-wrapped in the middle of the driveway. Confused, she put on her robe and ran out to the driveway, and brought the box back in the house. She opened it and found a brand new bathroom scale.

One day while going through a magazine, she came across an ad for a hair coloring product featuring a beautiful young model with hair a shade that she liked. Wanting a second opinion, she asked her husband, "Bruce, how do you think this color would look on a face with a few wrinkles?" Bruce looked at the picture, crumbled it up, straightened it out and studied it again. "Just great, honey."

My wife said, "You always carry my photo in your wallet, even after all these years of marriage" I responded, "When there is a problem, no matter how impossible, I look at your picture and the problem disappears." She grinned, "You see how miraculous and powerful I am for you?" Then I said, "Yes! I see your picture and ask myself what other problem can there be greater than this one?"

When our lawn mower broke and wouldn't run, my wife kept hinting to me that I should get it fixed. But, somehow I always had something else to take care of first, the truck, the car, playing golf. I always found something more important to me. Finally she thought of a clever way to make her point. When I arrived home one day, I found her seated in the tall grass, busily snipping away with a tiny pair of sewing scissors. I watched silently for a short time and then went into the house. I was gone only a minute, and when I came out again I handed her a toothbrush. I said, 'When you finish cutting the grass, you might as well sweep the driveway.

Charlie had just finished reading a new book entitled, 'YOU CAN BE THE MAN OF YOUR HOUSE'. He stormed up to his wife in the kitchen and announced, 'From now on, you need to know that I am the man of this house and my word is Law. You will prepare me a delicious meal tonight, and when I'm finished eating my meal, you will serve me a sumptuous dessert. After dinner, you are going to go upstairs with me and you will make love to me. Afterwards, you are going to draw me a bath so I can relax. You will wash my back and towel me dry and bring me my robe. Then, you will massage my feet and hands. Then tomorrow, guess who's going to dress me and comb my hair?' His wife replied, 'The funeral director would be my first guess. .

I was annoyed when my wife told me that a car had backed into her, damaging a fender, and that she hadn't gotten the license number. "What kind of car was he driving?" I asked. "I don't know," she said. "I never can tell one car from another." At that, I decided the time had come to teach her, and for the next few days, whenever I was driving with her, I made her name each car they passed until I was satisfied that she could recognize every make. It worked. I was driving her to the doctor's office when she exclaimed with a pleased expression on her face. "Dan," she said. "I hit a Toyota!"

Every Saturday morning Clint is going fishing. He gets up early and eager, makes his lunch, hooks up his boat and off he goes...all day long. Well, one Saturday morning he gets up early, dresses quietly, gets his lunch made, puts on his long johns, grabs the dog and goes to the garage to hook up his boat to the truck and down the driveway he goes. Coming out of his garage the rain is pouring down; it is like a torrential downpour. There is snow mixed in with the rain, and the wind is blowing 50 mph. Minutes later, he returns to the garage. He comes back into the house and turns the TV to the weather channel. He finds it's going to be bad weather all day long, so he puts his boat back in the garage, quietly undresses and slips back into bed. Then Clint cuddles up to his wife's back, now with a different anticipation, and whispers, "The weather out there is terrible." To which she sleepily replies" Can you believe my stupid husband is out fishing in this weather?"

We had another argument over something stupid and my wife threw me out. When I got home from work I discovered that she packed my bags, and as I walked out the front door, she screamed, "I wish you a slow and painful death, you bastard!" "Oh," I replied, "so now you want me to stay!"

Having been married ten years and still living in an apartment, Pam would often complain about anything, as she was tired of saving every penny just to buy a "dream home". Trying to placate her, Rob found a new home, something that was within their budget. However, after the first week, she began complaining again. "Honey," she said, "I don't like this place at all. There are no curtains in the bathroom. The neighbors can see me every time I take a bath". "Don't worry," Rob replied, "If the neighbors do see you, they'll buy curtains."

We were lying in bed late one night and I whispered to my wife, "if I died, would you get married again?" "I suppose so," she replied. "Would you sleep in the same bed with him?""Well, it's the only bed in the house, so I have no choice." "Would you make love to him?" "Honey," she said patiently, "he would be my husband." "Would you give him my car?" "No," she yawned, "He can't drive a stick shift."

Ivan said to his wife, "When I get mad at you, you never fight back. How do you control your anger? His wife said, "I clean the toilet" Ivan asked, "How does that help?" His wife smiled as she replied, "I use your toothbrush".

My wife and I were sitting at a table at her high school reunion, and she kept staring at a drunken man swigging his drink as he sat alone at a nearby table. I asked her, 'Do you know him? "Yes, ' she sighed, 'He's my old boyfriend. I understand he took to drinking right after we split up those many years ago, and I hear he hasn't been sober since. I said, 'Who would think that a person could go on celebrating that long? '

Halfway through a romantic dinner out, her husband smiled and said, "You look so beautiful under these lights." She was falling in love all over again when he added, "We have to get some of these lights."

"Honey," Roger said to his wife, "I invited a friend home for supper tonight." "What? Are you crazy? The house is a mess, I didn't go shopping, all the dishes are dirty, and I don't feel like cooking a fancy meal!" "I know all that." Roger replied. "Then why did you invite a friend for supper?" Roger responded, "Because the poor fool's thinking about getting married."

Gina is feeling poorly and sends a telegram to her husband who is on a business trip asking him to come home as soon as possible, "NOT GETTING ANY BETTER. COME HOME." Imagine her husband's surprise when he received this telegram, "NOT GETTING ANY. BETTER COME HOME."

Martha had gained a few pounds recently. It was most noticeable to her when she squeezed into a pair of her old blue jeans. Wondering if the added weight was noticeable to everyone else, she asked her husband, "Steve, do these jeans make me look like the side of the house?" "No, dear, not at all," he replied, "Our house isn't blue."

Jessica goes into a sporting goods store to buy a shotgun. "It's for my husband," she tells the clerk. "Did he tell you what gauge to get?" asked the clerk. "Are you kidding?" she says. "He doesn't even know that I'm going to shoot him!"

My wife asked me, "What do you like most in me, my pretty face or my sexy body?" I looked at her from head to toe and replied, "I like your sense of humor."

My wife called yesterday and said, "The car won't start, but I know what the problem is." I asked her what she thought it was, and she told me there was water in the carburetor. I thought for a moment, her car has fuel injection. "No, there's definitely water in the carburetor," she insisted. "OK Kathy, that's fine, I'll just go take a look. Where is the car?" She replied, "In the lake."

Nick went shopping with his wife for some clothes for their vacation, and they passed a display of bathing suits. It had been at least twenty years and forty pounds since she had even considered purchasing a bathing suit, so she asked Nick's advice. "What do you think?" She asked. "Should I get a bikini or a one piece?" "You'd better get a bikini," Nick replied. "You'd never fit it all in one." Has anyone seen Nick lately?

My wife worked as a beautician, and sometimes she had to work with people who were visually handicapped, which is the politically correct term for ugly. This one woman asked, "When you're finished with me, will my husband think I'm beautiful? My wife muttered under her breath, "Maybe. Does he still drink a lot?"

Mark and Linda are shopping in a supermarket when he picks up a 12 pack of beer and sticks it in the carriage. "What do you think you're doing?" "They're on special offer, only $ 10 for 12 cans," "Put them back. We can't afford it." And they carry on shopping. A bit later, Linda picks up a jar of face cream and sticks it in the carriage. "What do you think you're doing?" asks Mark. "It's my face cream. It makes me look beautiful." She says. And then Mark responded, "So do 12 cans of beer and it's half the price."

Claudia awakes during the night to find that her husband was not in bed. She puts on her robe and goes downstairs to look for him. She finds him sitting at the dining room table with a cup of coffee in front of him. She watches as he wipes a tear from his eye and takes a sip of coffee. "What's the matter, dear?" she whispers as she steps into the room. "Why are you down here at this time of night?" Her husband looks up, "Do you remember 40 years ago when we were dating, and you were only 18?" he asks solemnly. Claudia is touched to tears thinking that her husband is so caring and sensitive. "Yes, I do," she replies. Her husband pauses. The words are not coming easily. "Do you remember when your father caught us on the couch making love?" "Yes, I remember." She says, lowering herself into a chair beside him. Her husband continues..."Do you remember when he shoved a shotgun in my face and said, 'Either you marry my daughter, or I will send you to jail for 40 years?'" "I remember that, too." she replies softly. He wipes another tear from his cheek and says "I would have gotten out today"

Chapter 15. Anniversary's Aren't All Happy

In a stationery store, Mike spent a half-hour searching for the right anniversary card for his wife. Noticing he was lingering over one card after another, the pretty young clerk went to see if she could help. "Is there a problem?" she asked. "Yes, there is," he replied ruefully. "I can't find one my wife will believe."

The couple's 50th wedding anniversary was approaching. The husband asked his long-suffering wife, "What would you like to do for our anniversary, Dear?" She looked at him sourly and replied, "Become a widow!"

Bob and Nancy were married for 40 years and decided they wanted to renew their vows and planned a second wedding. They were discussing the details with their friends. Nancy wasn't going to wear a traditional bridal gown and she started describing the dress she was planning to wear. One of her friends asked what color shoes she had to go with the dress. She replied, "Silver." At that point, her husband chimed in, "Yep silver...to match her hair." Shooting a glaring look at Bob's bald spot, Nancy said, "So, Bob, I guess you are going barefoot."

On their 40th wedding anniversary and during the banquet celebrating it, Harley was asked to give his friends a brief account of the benefits of a marriage of such long duration. "Tell us Harley, just what is it you have learned from all those wonderful years with your wife?" Harley responds, "Well, I've learned that marriage is the best teacher of all. It teaches you loyalty, meekness, and self-restraint, forgiveness – and a great many other qualities you wouldn't have needed if you'd stayed single."

During their silver anniversary party, Steve and Polly were reminiscing and she asked her husband, "Do you remember when you proposed to me, I was so overwhelmed that I didn't talk for an hour?" He thought back to that moment, and then Steve replied, "Yes, honey, that was the happiest hour of my life."

A husband and wife were celebrating their 80th wedding anniversary, which is quite an accomplishment. The media was there to document the occasion. One of the reporters asked the secret to their successful marriage and longevity. The wife replied that they had never been sick. The young reporter was astonished and to confirm that he said, "So, you've never been bedridden." And the wife quickly replied, "Oh, hundreds of times, and twice in a buggy."

A couple was being interviewed on their Golden Wedding Anniversary. "In all that time, did you ever consider divorce?" they were asked." "Oh, no, not divorce," one said. "Murder sometimes, but never divorce."

On their 25th anniversary, Dale took his wife to dinner. Their teenage daughters told them that they would have dessert waiting for them when they returned. After the couple got home, they saw that the dining room table was beautifully set, and there was a note that read, "Your dessert is in the refrigerator. We are staying with friends, so go ahead and do something we wouldn't do!" "I suppose we could vacuum..." Dale said.

One bright, beautiful Sunday morning, everyone in the tiny town of Johnstown got up early and went to the local church. Before the services started, the townspeople were sitting in their pews. Suddenly, Satan appeared at the front of the Church. Everyone started screaming and running for the front entrance, trampling each other in a frantic effort to get away from Evil Incarnate. Soon everyone was evacuated from the Church; except for one elderly gentleman who sat calmly in his pew, not moving . . .Now this confused Satan a bit, so he walked up to the man and said, "Don't you know who I am?" The man replied, "Yup, sure do."Satan asked, "Well, aren't you afraid of me?" "Nope, sure ain't," said the man. Satan was more than a little perturbed at this and queried, "Why not?" The man calmly replied, "Been married to your sister for over 48 years!"

Doug and Sharon were about to celebrate their 20 year anniversary but instead they had an awful fight and went to bed that night not saying a word to each other. The next morning, Doug felt really bad about the argument and apologized to Sharon, hoping to smooth things over. "Honey" he said, "I'm really sorry I ruined our anniversary. Please forgive me." Sharon said, "Okay, you're forgiven, yet again" Doug asked, "You're the best babe. You don't regret marrying me, do you?" Sharon sighed, "Every second of my life!"

At my granddaughter's wedding, the singer for the band polled the guests to see who had been married longest. It turned out to be my uncle and his wife. He asked them, "What advice would you give to the newly-married couple?" My aunt Carole said, "The three most important words in a marriage are, 'You're probably right.'" Everyone then looked at my uncle Harley. He said, "She's probably right."

Chapter 16. Senior Citizens

My dad is 90 and he's been married for 67 years to my mother. He told me that his mother in law only agreed with him on one thing- That he shouldn't have married her daughter.

A Doctor was addressing a large audience in Jacksonville, Florida. "The food we put into our stomachs is hazardous enough to have killed most of us sitting here. Red meat is awful. Soft drinks corrode your stomach lining. But there is one thing that is the most dangerous of all and we all have, or will, eat it. Can anyone here tell me what food it is that causes the most grief and suffering after eating it?" After several seconds of quiet, a 75-year-old man in the front row raised his hand, and softly said, "Wedding Cake."

An 80 year old woman was arrested for shop lifting. When she went before the judge he asked her, "What did you steal?" She replied: a can of peaches. The judge asked her why she had stolen them and she replied that she was hungry. The judge then asked her how many peaches were in the can. She replied "six". The judge then said, "I will give you six days in jail." Before the judge could actually pronounce the punishment the woman's husband spoke up and asked the judge if he could say something. He said, "What is it?" The husband said "She also stole a can of peas."

Because they had no reservations at a busy restaurant, my elderly neighbor and his wife were told there would be a 45 minute wait for a table. "Young man, we're both 90 years old," the husband said. "We may not have 45 minutes." They were seated immediately.

On an airplane, I overheard a stewardess talking to an elderly couple seated in the same row across from me. Learning that it was the couple's 50th wedding anniversary, the flight attendant congratulated them and asked how they had done it. "It all felt like five minutes..." the gentleman said slowly. The stewardess had just begun to remark on what a sweet statement that was when he finished his sentence with a word that earned him a sharp smack on the head: "...underwater."

While waiting to register at a hotel, I overheard the couple ahead of me asking for a room with a king, queen or double bed. The clerk apologized and said that the only rooms available had twin beds. Disappointed, the man remarked, "I don't know. We've been sharing the same bed for 44 years." "Could you possibly put them close together?" the wife asked. Several people nearby smiled, and someone commented, "How romantic." Then the woman finished her request with, "Because if he snores, I want to be able to punch him."

Edith was a little old lady was sitting on a park bench in The Pines, a Florida adult community. A man walked over and sits down on the other end of the bench. After a few moments, the woman asks, "Are you a stranger here?" He replies, "I lived here many years ago." She inquired, "So, where were you all these years?" "In prison," he says. "Why did they put you in prison?" He looked at her, and very quietly said, "I killed my wife." "Oh!" said Edith. "So you're single..."

An elderly couple had a parlor in which they kept a couple of food bins. One of those bins contained apples, and the other bin contained nuts. They were having quite a bit of trouble with mice, so one evening before going to bed they set a couple of mouse traps, one by the bin of apples and one by the bin of nuts. During the night they heard a trap snap. The old gentleman got up to see which mouse trap had caught a mouse. On returning to bed his wife asked, "Well did we catch him by the apples?" The old gentleman replied, "Nope, guess again."

An elderly couple, Elmer and Edith, were sitting together on their front porch. "You used to sit closer to me," said Edith. So Elmer moved closer. "You used to put your arm around me." So Elmer put his arm around her. "You used to nibble on my ear." "Okay, I will be right back. Let me get my teeth."

One evening there was a community supper in the Club House, and the widower and widow made a foursome with two other singles. They had a wonderful evening and spirits were high. The widower sent a few admiring glances across the table, and the widow smiled coyly back at him. Finally, he plucked up his courage to ask her, "Will you marry me?" After about six seconds of careful consideration, she answered, "Yes. Yes, I will. " The meal ended with a few more pleasant exchanges and they went to their respective homes. The next morning, the widower was troubled. Did she say 'Yes', or did she say 'No'? He couldn't remember. Try as he would, he just could not recall. He went over the conversation of the previous evening, but his mind was blank. He remembered asking the question, but for the life of him he could not recall her response. With fear and trepidation, he picked up the phone and called her. First, he explained that he didn't remember as well as he used to. Then he reviewed the lovely evening past. As he gained a little more courage he then inquired of her, "When I asked if you would marry me, did you say 'Yes' or did you say 'No'?" "Why, you silly man, I said 'Yes. Yes I will.' And I meant it with all my heart. "The widower was delighted. He felt his heart skip a beat. Then she continued, "And I am so glad you called because I couldn't remember who asked me."

Alice and George were in their late 70's. They had married as childhood sweethearts and had moved back to their old neighborhood after they retired. Holding hands, they walked back to their old school. It was unlocked, so they entered, and found the old desk where George had carved "George and Alice." On their way back home, a bag of money fell out of an armored car, practically landing at their feet. Alice quickly picked it up, but not sure what to do with it, they took it home. There, she counted the money -- fifty-thousand dollars. George said, "We've got to give it back." Alice said, "Finders keepers." She put the money back in the bag and hid it in their attic. The next day, two FBI men were canvassing the neighborhood looking for the money. They and knocked on Alice and George's door. "Pardon me, but did either of you find a bag that fell out of an armored car yesterday?" Alice said, "No." George said, "She's lying. She hid it up in the attic." Alice said, "Don't believe him, he's getting senile." The agents began to question George. One says: "Tell us the story from the beginning. George starts, "Well, when Alice and I were walking home from school yesterday . . ." The first FBI guy turns to his partner and says, "We're outta here!"

George approached an attractive younger woman at a shopping mall. 'Excuse me; I can't seem to find my wife. Can you talk to me for a couple of minutes?' The woman, feeling a bit of compassion for the old fellow, said, 'Of course, sir. Do you know where your wife might be?' 'I have no idea, but every time I talk to a beautiful young woman, she appears out of nowhere.'

A man and a woman had been married for more than 60 years. They had shared everything. They had kept no secrets from each other except that the little old woman had a shoe box in the top of her closet that she had cautioned her husband never to open or ask her about. For all of these years, he had never thought about the box, but one day the little old woman got very sick and the doctor said she would not recover. In trying to sort out their affairs, the little old man took down the shoe box and took it to his wife's bedside. She agreed that it was time that he should know what was in the box. When he opened it, he found two crocheted dolls and a stack of money totaling $95,000. He asked her about the contents. "When we were to be married," she said, "my grandmother told me the secret of a happy marriage was to never argue. She told me that if I ever got angry with you, I should just keep quiet and crochet a doll." The little old man was so moved; he had to fight back tears. Only two precious dolls were in the box. She had only been angry with him two times in all those years of living and loving. He almost burst with happiness. "Honey," he said "that explains the doll, but what about all of this money? Where did it come from?" "Oh, that?" she said. "That's the money I made from selling the dolls."

Mary and Wayne decided to fly her elderly father in to see them for Christmas. Immediately after he landed a blizzard blanketed the city with snow and they could not get to the airport to pick him up. The people at the airport were kind enough to help with the accommodations and got him on a cab to his motel.

After checking in, he went to his room and was back within minutes. He complained, "My room is too small and it doesn't have a TV or a bathroom." The attendant at the desk followed him to his room and he kindly explained that it was the elevator, not his room.

An elderly couple had dinner at another couple's house, and after eating, the wives left the table and went into the kitchen. The two gentlemen were talking, and one said, 'Last night we went out to a new restaurant and it was really great. I would recommend it very highly. 'The other man said, 'What is the name of the restaurant? The first man thought and thought and finally said, what is the name of that flower you give to someone you love? You know the flower that's red and has thorns. "Do you mean a rose? "Yes, that's the one, ' replied the man. He then turned towards the kitchen and yelled, 'Rose, what's the name of that restaurant we went to last night?

One evening while we were dining in a restaurant, a waiter strode through our section asking, "Does anyone here drive a silver New Yorker?" We assumed its headlights had been left on. "Yes!" an elderly gentleman in a neighboring booth responded emphatically. His wife reacted instantly. "Henry! You don't drive a silver New Yorker!" Looking chagrined, he replied, "Oh, I thought the waiter said, 'Is anyone here ready to order?'"

Russell and Mabel, who are in their 90's are both having problems remembering things. During a checkup, the doctor tells them that they're physically okay, but t hey might want to start writing things down to help them remember. Later that night, while watching TV, the old man gets up from his chair. 'Want anything while I'm in the kitchen? 'He asks. Will you get me a bowl of ice cream? "Sure. "Don't you think you should write it down so you can remember it? 'She asks. 'No, I can remember it. 'Well, I'd like some strawberries on top, too. Maybe you should write it down, so you won't forget it? '; He says, 'I can remember that. You want a bowl of ice cream with strawberries. 'I'd also like whipped cream. I'm certain you'll forget that, write it down? 'She asks. Irritated, he says, 'I don't need to write it down, I can remember it! Ice cream with strawberries and whipped cream - I got it, for goodness sake! 'Then he toddles into the kitchen. After about 20 minutes, the old man returns from the kitchen and hands his wife a plate of bacon and eggs. She stares at the plate for a moment. 'Where's my toast? '

Aunt Edna was talking to me the other day. She told me about my uncle Wally. "We were married for forty-five years before he died," she said, dabbing away a tear. "We never had an argument in all those years." "Amazing," I said. "How did you do it?" She answered, "I outweighed him by forty pounds and he was a coward."

Chapter 17. Till Death Do Us Part

Tom and his wife Kathleen are in the park and they come up to a wishing well. Tom leans over, makes a wish, and throws in a penny. Kathleen decides to make a wish, too, but she leans over too far, falls into the well, and drowns. Tom says, "Wow...it works."

My wife and I were sitting around the breakfast table one lazy Sunday morning. I said to her, "If I were to die suddenly, I want you to immediately sell all my stuff." "Now why would you want me to do something like that?" she asked. "I figure that you would eventually remarry and I don't want some other jerk using my stuff." She looked at me and said: "What makes you think I'd marry another jerk?"

One of our neighbors is making interesting plans for the future. She says when her husband dies she's not going to have him buried. I said, "What are you going to do?" She said, "I'm not going to have him cremated, I'm going to have him stuffed and mounted and put on the living room couch. Then I'll turn on the TV to a football game, talk to him and he won't answer. It'll be just like he never left."

Jake was dying. His wife sat at the bedside. He looked up and said weakly: 'I have something I must confess.' 'There's no need to, 'his wife replied. 'No, ' he insisted, 'I want to die in peace. I slept with your sister, and your best friend.' 'I know, ' she replied, 'That's why I poisoned you.'

Now that they are retired, my mother and father are discussing all aspects of their future. "What will you do if I die before you do?" Dad asked Mom. After some thought, she said that she'd probably look for a house sharing situation with three other single or widowed women who might be a little younger than herself, since she is so active for her age. Then Mom asked Dad, "What will you do if I die first?" He replied, "Probably the same thing."

Grace was a talented local artist, and if her schedule allowed, she would paint portraits. Mrs. Swanson was one of her subjects and she had an unusual request. "Paint me with diamond earrings, a diamond necklace, emerald bracelets and a ruby pendant." "But you are not wearing any of those things." Grace protested. "I know," said Mrs. Swanson. "But my health is not good and my husband is having an affair with his secretary." "When I die, I'm sure he will marry her, and I want the bitch to go nuts looking for the jewelry."

A young woman is widowed after only a few years of marriage, and it is not long before her friends begin to ask her if she is thinking of marrying again. "Right now, no," the young woman answers. "I've hardly begun to enjoy using the remote control."

Rob goes to see his Rabbi. He says, "Rabbi, I think my wife is poisoning me." The Rabbi says, "I'll tell you what...let me talk to her. I'll see what I can find out and I'll let you know." A week later the Rabbi calls Rob and says, "I spoke to your wife on the phone for four hours." Rob says, "do you have any advice?" The Rabbi says, "Yeah. Take the poison."

Liz was told by her husband, "I've insured myself for $1,000,000. I just wanted you to know at if anything happens to me you will be provided for." "Good," replied Liz, "Now you won't have to call the doctor every time you feel sick."

I was telling one of my friends at work, "I've been married for almost forty years, and believe me, it hasn't been easy. By way of comparison, forty years is longer than most murderers spend in jail"

Jack decided to go skiing with his buddy, Bob. So they loaded up Jack's minivan and headed north. After driving for a few hours, they got caught in a terrible blizzard. So they pulled into a nearby farm and asked the attractive lady who answered the door if they could spend the night. "I realize it is terrible weather out there and I have this huge house all to myself, but I'm recently widowed," she explained. "I'm afraid the neighbors will talk if I let you stay in my house." "Don't worry," Jack said. "We'll be happy to sleep in the barn. And if the weather breaks, we'll be gone at first light." The lady agreed, and the two men found their way to the barn and settled in for the night. Come morning, the weather had cleared, and they got on their way. About nine months later, Jack got an unexpected letter from an attorney. It took him a few minutes to figure it out, but he finally determined that it was from the attorney of that attractive widow he had met on the ski weekend. He dropped in on his friend Bob and asked, "Bob, do you remember that good-looking widow from the farm we stayed at on our ski holiday up north about 9 months ago?" "Yes, I do." said Bob. "Did you happen to get up in the middle of the night and pay her a visit?" "Well, um, yes," Bob said, a little embarrassed about being found out. "I have to admit that I did." "And did you happen to use my name instead of telling her your name?" Bob's face turned beet red and he said, "Yeah, look, I'm sorry, buddy. I'm afraid I did." Why do you ask?" "She just died and left me everything."

The old man had died. A wonderful funeral was in progress and the country preacher talked at length of the good traits of the deceased; what an honest man he was, what a loving husband and kind father he had been. The widow meanwhile was ever so slightly shaking her head, as she intently listened to the preacher's words. Finally, the widow leaned over and whispered to one of her children.... "Erica, honey, go on up there and take a look in the coffin and see if that's your pa in there."

A man charges into a bank wearing a mask and wielding a loaded handgun. He shouts "this is a robbery – everyone get on the floor!", and proceeds to empty the cash drawers. As he runs towards the door with the loot, a brave customer yanks off his mask. The robber immediately shoots the customer and shouts "did anyone else here see my face?" The robber notices another customer peering from behind a counter and goes over and shoots him also. "Did anyone else see my face?" he shouts again, waving his gun around. There is silence for a few seconds before a male voice is heard from a distant corner.... "I think my wife caught a glimpse......"

His wife's graveside service was just barely finished, when there was a massive clap of thunder, followed by tremendous bolt of lightning, accompanied by even more thunder rumbling in the distance. The little old man looked at the pastor and calmly said, 'Well, she's there.

Made in the USA
Lexington, KY
13 January 2014